The Circulatory System

CHRISTINE TAYLOR-BUTLER

Children's Press®
An Imprint of Scholastic Inc.
New York   Toronto   London   Auckland   Sydney
Mexico City   New Delhi   Hong Kong
Danbury, Connecticut

Content Consultant

Lawrence J. Cheskin, M.D., F.A.C.P.
Associate Professor of Medicine
Johns Hopkins University School of Medicine
Baltimore, Maryland

Library of Congress Cataloging-in-Publication Data

Taylor-Butler, Christine.
　The Circulatory system / by Christine Taylor-Butler.
　　　p. cm. -- (A true book)
　Includes bibliographical references and index.
　　ISBN-13: 978-0-531-16856-1 (lib. bdg.)
　　　　　　978-0-531-20730-7 (pbk.)
　　ISBN-10: 0-531-16856-5 (lib. bdg.)
　　　　　　0-531-20730-7 (pbk.)

1. Cardiovascular system--Juvenile literature. I. Title. II. Series.

　QP103.T39 2008
　612.1--dc22　　　　　　　　2007036019

Produced by Weldon Owen Education Inc.

1 2 3 4 5 6 7 8 9 10 R 17 16 15 14 13 12 11 10 09 08

Find the Truth!

Everything you are about to read is true **except** for one of the sentences on this page.

Which one is **TRUE**?

T or F Red blood cells deliver carbon dioxide to your lungs.

T or F The right side of your heart does most of the work.

Find the answers in this book.

3

Contents

THE **BIG** TRUTH!

Let's Circulate!

You can lose as much as 25 percent of your blood and still survive.

Skipping rope is a great way to keep fit. It also improves your flexibility and coordination.

CHAPTER 1

Keep Up the Beat

It's the final round of the double Dutch contest. You've saved your best moves for last. You jump and do a handstand as the ropes whip by. Your heart pounds in your chest as you finish your routine. You are breathing hard. Your face is flushed. Your circulatory system is in action. That's a good thing!

Skipping for ten minutes is the equivalent of running one mile (1.6 kilometers) in eight minutes.

Your heart acts as a pump to move blood to every part of your body. The blood circulates inside a series of tubes, or blood vessels. These vessels reach from the top of your head to the tips of your fingers and toes.

Your blood carries oxygen from your lungs to the rest your body. It also removes **carbon dioxide** from your cells. It returns the carbon dioxide to your lungs so that you can breathe it out.

The circulatory system works 24 hours a day, seven days a week. It works even when you are sleeping.

At rest, an adult's heart pumps about 11 pints (5 liters) of blood each minute. During exercise, this rate can rise to as high as 70 pints (35 liters) a minute.

The circulatory system works with other systems and organs in your body. It delivers food, chemicals, and fluids to cells throughout your body. It helps rid your body of waste. It carries cells that fight disease. If your circulatory system stopped working, your cells would starve. You would soon die.

Sometimes medicine is injected directly into a patient's circulatory system. The medicine travels to parts of the body that need it.

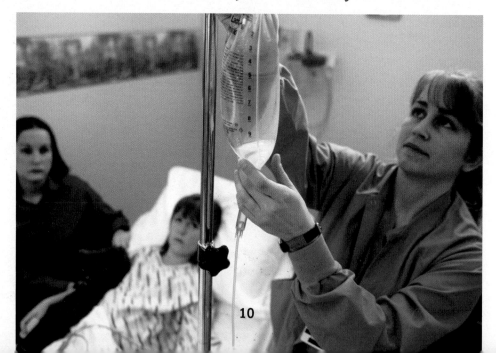

10

The Air Up There

Mount Everest is the world's highest mountain. It is 29,035 feet (8,850 meters) above sea level. At sea level, oxygen makes up about 21 percent of the air. At the top of Mount Everest, oxygen is still 21 percent of the air. However, the air pressure is about a third of what it is at sea level. As a result, climbers take in less oxygen with each breath. This can cause dizziness, headaches, and tiredness. It can even lead to death. That is why mountain climbers often carry extra oxygen in tanks.

Arteries and veins are connected by capillaries. In diagrams, arteries are often shown as red. Veins are often shown as blue.

Capillaries

Artery

Vein

Heart

CHAPTER 2

Your Round-Trip Ticket

The circulatory system consists of three main parts: the heart, the blood vessels, and the blood. Your heart and blood vessels form a loop in your body. Your blood makes one round trip after another within this closed loop. The two main kinds of blood vessels are the **arteries** and **veins**. There are also smaller vessels called **capillaries**.

Arteries and veins run parallel through the body.

Get Into the Rhythm

The human heart is a muscle. It is about the size of your fist. **Nerves** in the heart automatically control the contraction, or squeezing, of the heart.

The heart has a left side and a right side. Blood enters the heart from the body on the right side. Then it goes from the right side of the heart to the lungs. There it picks up oxygen. It returns to the left side of the heart. The oxygen-rich blood is then pumped to the body. The heart contains **valves**. The valves keep the blood flowing in one direction.

Each side of the heart is divided into two parts. The upper chamber is called an atrium. It receives blood from veins. The lower chamber is called a ventricle. It delivers blood to the arteries. When the walls of the ventricles contract, blood is forced out of the chamber.

How the Heart Pumps Blood

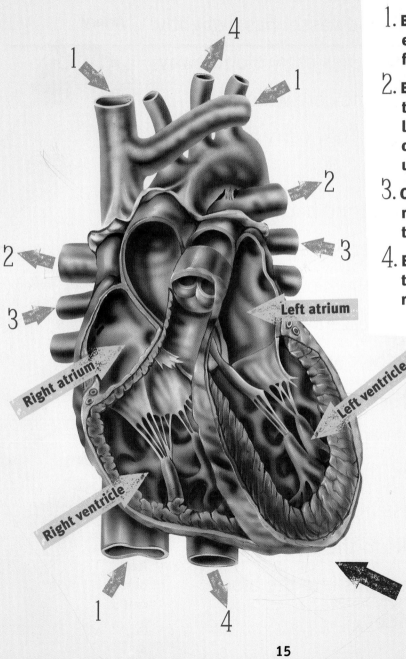

1. **Blood in need of oxygen enters the right atrium from the body.**

2. **Blood is pumped from the right ventricle to the lungs. There it drops off carbon dioxide and picks up oxygen.**

3. **Oxygen-rich blood returns from the lungs to the left atrium**

4. **Blood is pumped from the left ventricle to the rest of the body.**

Left atrium

Right atrium

Left ventricle

Right ventricle

The left side of the heart is bigger than the right. This is because it does more work.

15

Get Circulating

Each type of blood vessel has a slightly different job. Arteries carry blood away from the heart. They are wide. They have thick walls. They carry a lot of blood at high pressure.

Artery

Veins carry blood back to the heart. They have thinner walls than arteries. This is because the blood inside them is under lower pressure. Veins have valves inside their walls to keep blood from flowing backward.

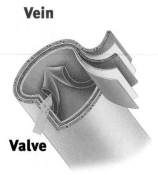

Vein

Valve

Capillaries are narrower than a human hair. They have thin walls. Nutrients pass from the blood through capillary walls to the cells. Wastes pass from the cells into the blood in the capillaries.

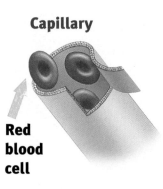

Capillary

Red blood cell

When you exercise, your circulatory system helps you cool down. It pumps more blood than usual through the vessels close to your skin. This allows heat to escape from your body. If you have fair skin, this makes your skin appear flushed.

An adult human heart beats about 100,000 times a day.

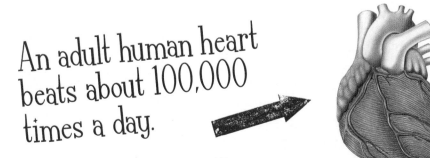

Red, White, and Platelets

Your blood contains billions of cells. These cells are made inside your bones in a substance called bone marrow. Most of the cells are red blood cells. Their main task is to carry oxygen. The iron and oxygen in red blood cells combine to give blood its red color.

White blood cells are the body's defense system. They seek out and destroy foreign substances, such as germs, that invade the body.

Platelets are tiny cells. They help form a clot over a wound to stop the body from losing blood. A clot also keeps out germs.

How a Wound Heals

1.
Ouch! You've cut yourself. Blood rushes out of the wound.

2.
Platelets and sticky fibers trap red blood cells and germs. A clot is formed that seals the leak.

Skin

Bloodstream

White blood cell

Platelet

Red blood cells

The liquid part of blood isn't red. It's a colorless fluid called plasma. It is mostly water. Blood is about 54 percent plasma, 45 percent red blood cells, and 1 percent white blood cells and platelets. In a drop of blood the size of a pinhead, there are about 5 million red blood cells, 10,000 white blood cells, and 250,000 platelets.

3.
When the clot dries, it becomes a scab. Cells multiply to make new skin.

4.
Capillaries under the skin reseal. The scab falls off when the wound is healed.

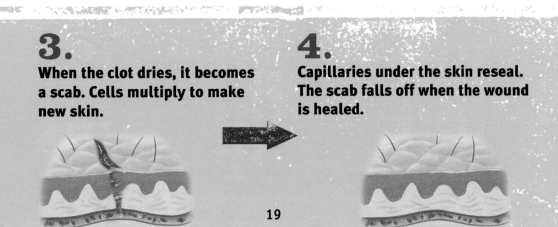

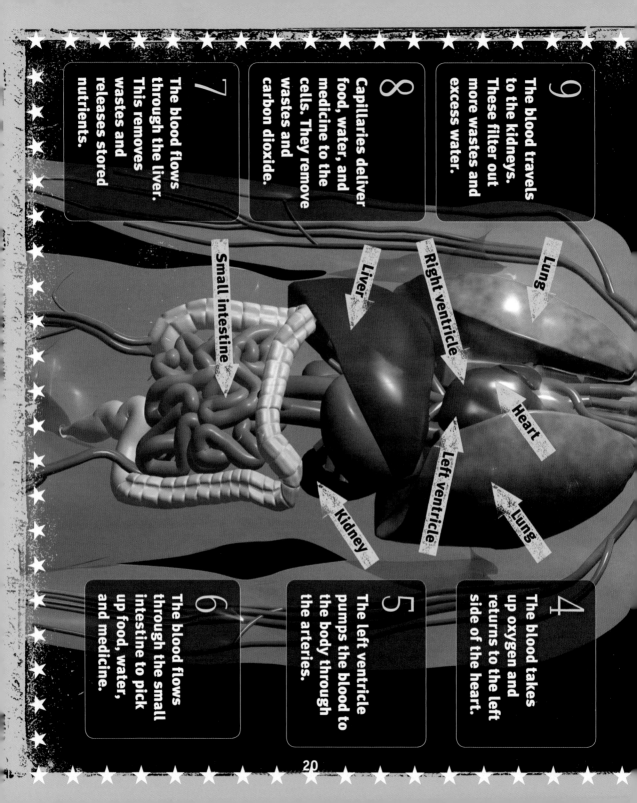

9 The blood travels to the kidneys. These filter out more wastes and excess water.

8 Capillaries deliver food, water, and medicine to the cells. They remove wastes and carbon dioxide.

7 The blood flows through the liver. This removes wastes and releases stored nutrients.

Small intestine

Liver

Right ventricle

Lung

Heart

Left ventricle

Lung

Kidney

4 The blood takes up oxygen and returns to the left side of the heart.

5 The left ventricle pumps the blood to the body through the arteries.

6 The blood flows through the small intestine to pick up food, water, and medicine.

Let's Circulate!

Your heart is a fantastic pumping machine. It takes about a minute to circulate blood to every cell in your body. Your heart works even faster when you are exercising. Other organs in your body also help with circulation.

1
Blood enters the heart on the right side.

10
Veins return the blood to the heart so that the process can start all over again.

2
The right ventricle pumps blood to the lungs.

3
The lungs remove carbon dioxide from the blood.

CHAPTER 3

Getting a Tune-Up

A checkup from your doctor is a good way to make sure that your body is working well. Your doctor may check your pulse. He or she places two fingers on an artery and counts the beats. Your heartbeat will be checked with a **stethoscope**. Your blood pressure might be measured using a special cuff that wraps around your arm.

Stethoscope comes from the Greek words *stéthos* and *skopé,* meaning "chest" and "examination."

Making Blood Better

Sometimes a coronary (heart) artery becomes clogged. That happens when fatty material builds up inside the artery. This makes it harder for blood to circulate. Doctors can insert a small tube into a clogged artery. The tube contains a special type of balloon. When the balloon inflates, it flattens the fatty material. This creates more space for the blood to pass through. This procedure is called **angioplasty**.

Angioplasty

An artery becomes clogged with fat.

A balloon is inserted into the artery.

The balloon inflates. The blockage is pushed out.

The balloon is removed. A soft wire frame remains to keep the artery open.

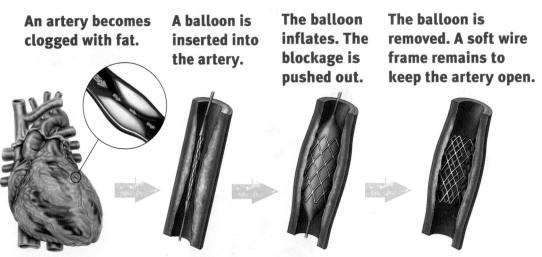

If a clogged artery is not fixed in time, the heart won't get enough blood. That could cause a heart attack. If an artery is too damaged to repair, the doctor can sew on a section of blood vessel taken from elsewhere in the body. This creates a new path for the blood to flow through. It bypasses the damaged area.

Sometimes the heart cannot be saved. In that case, a person will need a heart transplant. Hearts are donated from people who have recently died and whose blood type matches that of the patient.

In some cases, an artificial heart is implanted when a human donor heart is not available.

Blood Suckers

More than 2,500 years ago, leeches were used in ancient Egypt and ancient China to suck blood from a sick person. It was believed that bad blood caused many illnesses. The ancient Greeks and Romans also used leeches to drain blood when they believed a person had too much blood.

Recently, doctors have started using leeches again. Slimy leeches release a chemical called hirudin. This chemical prevents blood from clotting. It helps blood flow to damaged tissue. This makes leeches useful after surgery. Leeches also release a chemical that keeps a wound from feeling painful.

Leeches attach to the body with a sucker. Inside the sucker are about 100 tiny teeth.

Medical leeches are raised
in special laboratories.
This ensures that they do
not carry diseases.

If you have a fever, it is a sign that your body is fighting off an infection. A thermometer is used to measure body temperature.

CHAPTER 4

Your Automatic Pilot

Your body can combat minor infections without your even knowing about them. When the problem is more serious, your body can send you clues that you need to go to the doctor. Normally, the system that protects you from disease is at work continually. This system is called the immune system.

A normal body temperature is about 98.6°F (37°C). Anything higher than 100.5°F (38°C) is considered a fever.

White blood cells are part of both the circulatory system and the immune system. These cells are your body's first line of defense. When a germ enters the body, the white blood cells seek it out right away. Some white blood cells produce antibodies that destroy germs. Others surround germs and digest them.

Kinds of White Blood Cells

A macrophage (MAK-roh-fahj) is the largest white blood cell. It absorbs invaders.

A T cell finds invaders. Then it multiplies and attacks the invaders with chemicals.

A neutrophil (NU-truh-fil) attacks any foreign cells.

A B cell releases antibodies that allow macrophages to recognize invaders.

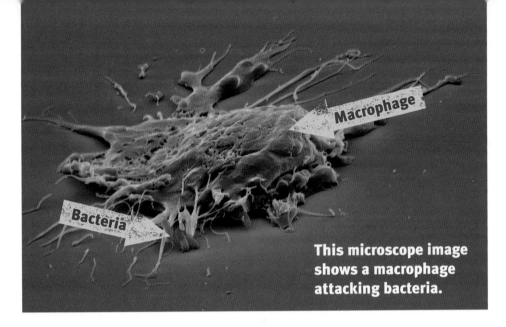

Macrophage

Bacteria

This microscope image shows a macrophage attacking bacteria.

 White blood cells live for only a few hours or days. Red blood cells can live for as long as four months.

Some people have serious illnesses that require a new organ or new blood from a donor. The donated part must be a close match. If it is not, the person's white blood cells will reject the replacement. The cells will treat it as a foreign substance. They will attack and destroy it. Special drugs often help prevent that from happening.

You can train your body to attack specific invaders. This is what you are doing when you get a shot called a vaccination. A vaccination contains weak or dead germs for a particular disease. Your body then creates antibodies from B cells. These antibodies recognize the invader and attach to it. The antibodies help white blood cells identify and destroy the germ. Your body is now able to produce lots of antibodies for that disease—you are immune to the disease. If you encounter that germ, you probably won't get sick. If you do, your illness will be less severe than it would have been.

A vaccination will make you immune to a particular disease, such as polio.

White Blood

Leukemia means "white blood." It is a form of cancer. It happens when the bone marrow makes too many white blood cells. These cells are not able to fight infection. They also crowd out normal red blood cells. This prevents the blood from carrying enough oxygen to the vital organs. A person with leukemia also has a lack of platelets in his or her blood. This means that the blood will not clot properly when there is a wound.

Some patients with leukemia undergo a treatment that destroys their bone marrow. Then they must get a transplant from someone who is a match for their blood type.

What's Your Type?

If you are badly injured or have surgery, you may lose a lot of blood. Your blood can be replaced with blood donated by other people. But the blood must be a good match for you.

Red blood cells may have chemicals on their surface called **antigens**. The two main antigens are A and B. Antigens determine blood type. All the red blood cells in a person's body have the same antigens. The cells may contain:

- A antigens (blood type A)
- B antigens (blood type B)
- both A and B antigens (blood type AB)
- neither A nor B antigens (blood type O)

Type A   **Type B**   **Type AB**   **Type O**

More than 15 million pints of blood are donated each year in the United States. The blood is labeled and stored in a blood bank.

There is another antigen called Rh. Blood is labeled positive (+) if it has the Rh antigen. It is labeled negative (−) if it does not.

People with type O− blood are called "universal donors." They can donate blood to anyone. People with type A blood can donate only to people who are A or AB. People with type B blood can donate only to people who are B or AB. People with type AB can only donate to other ABs. People with type AB+ blood are called "universal recipients." They can receive blood of any type.

You can get more fitness out of a walk by speedwalking or by walking up and down stairs.

CHAPTER 5

Pump Up the Volume

There are some easy ways to keep your circulatory system working well. Eat wisely and exercise often. Remember: your heart is a muscle. It gets stronger when it gets a workout. Any exercise that gets your heart pumping faster helps it remain strong and healthy.

A daily brisk walk of at least 30 minutes is one of the best ways to maintain fitness.

Healthy Eating Is the Key

When blood leaves the heart, it goes to the small intestine. It picks up nutrients from the food you have eaten. Fresh fruits, vegetables, and whole grains provide good nutrients for your body. Lean meats and fish are healthy too.

Some foods are bad for the circulatory system. Too much salt in your diet can lead to high blood pressure. This can damage the heart and blood vessels. Too many fats can clog your arteries. Being overweight also puts strain on the circulatory system.

Brush your teeth at least twice a day. The germs that cause plaque and gum disease have been linked to heart disease!

Check Your Pulse

Blood pressure is a measure of how much force the heart is using to push blood around the body. This force creates waves as the blood moves through your blood vessels. This is your heartbeat, or pulse.

The two easiest places to check your pulse are the neck and wrist. Place two fingers over an artery until you find a steady beat. Count the number of beats in 10 seconds. Then multiply that by six to get your beats per minute (bpm). At rest, a child's pulse is about 90 bpm. After exercising, it may be as rapid as 200 bpm.

The need for exercise is a good excuse to go out and play! Try to exercise at least 30 minutes a day—an hour is even better. As well as exercising and eating right, it is important to get plenty of rest.

If you take care of yourself, your heart and your circulatory system should last for a long, long time. ★

Amount of blood in adult body: Nearly 10 pints (5 liters)

Number of red blood cells in blood: 5 million per cubic millimeter

Number of white blood cells in blood: 10,000 per cubic millimeter

Number of white cells in the entire body: 40 billion

Number of platelets produced each day: 200 billion

Average lifespan of a red blood cell: 120 days

Average weight of human heart: 12 ounces (340 grams)

Amount of time brain can live without blood: About three minutes

Did you find the truth?

T Red blood cells deliver carbon dioxide to your lungs.

F The right side of your heart does most of the work.

Resources

Books

DK Publishing. *Alive: The Living Breathing Human Body Book*. New York: DK Children, 2007.

Glass, Susan. *The Circulatory System* (Reading Essentials in Science). Logan, IA: Perfection Learning, 2004.

Gray, Susan Heinrichs. *The Heart* (The Human Body). Mankato, MN: The Child's World, 2005.

Houghton, Gillian. *Blood: The Circulatory System* (Body Works). New York: Powerkids Press, 2006.

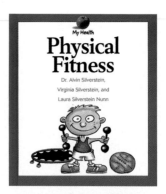

Parker, Steven, and Kristina Routh. *Heart, Blood and Lungs* (Understanding the Human Body). Strongsville, OH: Gareth Stevens Publishing, 2004.

Silverstein, Dr. Alvin and Virginia, and Laura Silverstein Nunn. *Physical Fitness* (My Health). New York: Franklin Watts, 2002.

Simon, Seymour. *The Heart: Our Circulatory System*. New York: HarperCollins, 2006.

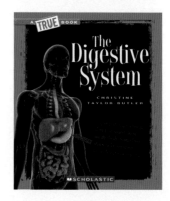

Taylor-Butler, Christine. *The Digestive System* (A True Book™: Health and the Human Body). New York: Children's Press, 2008.

Organizations and Web Sites

Get Body Smart

www.getbodysmart.com/ap/circulatory/menu/circulatory.html

View animations and do quizzes on the circulatory system.

Franklin Institute Resources for Science Learning

www.fi.edu/learn/heart/systems/circulation.html

This Web site has everything you need to know about the circulatory system.

ThinkQuest

http://library.thinkquest.org/5777/cir1.htm

Read an easy-to-follow guide to the circulatory system.

Places to Visit

The Franklin Institute Science Museum

222 North 20th Street
Philadelphia, PA 19103
215-448-1200
www2.fi.edu/exhibits/
permanent/giant-heart.php
Visit the giant heart and arteries interactive exhibition.

Science Museum of Minnesota

120 W. Kellogg Blvd.
St. Paul, MN 55102
651-221-9444
www.smm.org/heart/
humanBody
View the Bloodstream Superhighway in the Human Body Gallery.

Important Words

angioplasty (AN-jee-oh-plas-tee) – a medical procedure that clears a clogged artery

antibody – a substance in the blood that fights infection

antigen – a substance that triggers your immune system

artery (AR-tuh-ree) – a blood vessel that carries blood away from the heart

capillary (KAP-uh-lehr-ee) – a very thin blood vessel through which substances pass in and out of the bloodstream

carbon dioxide – a gas created by the body as a waste product

nerve – a bundle of specialized cells that carry messages to parts of the body such as muscles

platelet – a type of cell that helps wounds heal

stethoscope (STETH-uh-skope) – an instrument used to listen to the sounds from the heart, lungs, and other areas of the body

valve – a part of the heart and veins that allows blood to flow only in one direction

vein – a blood vessel that delivers blood to the heart

Index

About the Author

Christine Taylor-Butler lives in Kansas City, Missouri, with her husband and two daughters. A native of Ohio, she is the author of more than 40 books for children. She holds a B.S. degree in both Civil Engineering and Art and Design from the Massachusetts Institute of Technology in Cambridge, MA. Other books by Ms. Taylor-Butler in the True Book Health and the Human Body series include: *The Food Pyramid*, *Food Safety*, *Food Allergies*, *The Respiratory System*, *The Digestive System*, and *The Nervous System*.